THE GOLDFINCH
CAUTION TAPES

D1603646

THE GOLDFINCH
CAUTION TAPES

JAMES D'AGOSTINO

WAYWISER

First published in 2023 by

THE WAYWISER PRESS

Christmas Cottage, Church Enstone, Chipping Norton, Oxfordshire, OX7 4NN, UK
6419 Cedonia Avenue, Baltimore, MD 21206, USA
https://waywiser-press.com

Editor-in-Chief
Philip Hoy

Senior American Editor
Joseph Harrison

Associate Editors
Katherine Hollander | Eric McHenry | Dora Malech | V. Penelope Pelizzon
Clive Watkins | Greg Williamson | Matthew Yorke

Copyright © James D'Agostino, 2023

9 7 5 3 1 2 4 6 8

A CIP catalogue record for this book is available from the British Library

Paperback ISBN 978-1-911379-12-6

Printed and bound by
T. J. Books Limited, Padstow, Cornwall, PL28 8RW

Contents

FOREWORD BY ALICE FULTON   vii

Hello My Name   5
You Are   6
40°N, 92°W   8
Please Come   10
Prairie Warble   12
Last Sunday of Summer   13
Last Search   14
Quantum Tantrum   16
Evolutionary Aesthetic Safeguard   18
Attack Decay Sustain Release   19
Out Into the Worldness I Did Roam   20
The Goldfinch Caution Tapes   21
Kindled Measures Going Out   23
Besos de los Perros   24
This Foolishness About Moons and Blossoms   26
Bomb Threat Near the Library of Congress   28
Dear Amanda   29
Listing   31
Self-Portrait as Isaac Newton in Lockdown   34
Wake   36
Good Morning Night   37
1847   38
American Gothic   40
Derek Chauvin   41
Wiping My Ass with Your Kiss   43
Gorilla by Jellyfish Light   44
The Liberal Arts   45
Eureka   46
Mutually Assured Construction   48
With the Crew   50
Play Attention   51
I Am   53
Iron-Clad Lullaby   54
How Not to Float Off Into Space   55

Contents

Culled from the Lull 56
Estados Unidos 58
The Past Grows Steadily Around One ... 59
Ardor Vitae 61
Among the Attributes of a Basically Cruel Man 62
Immediately Dismissed from the Accident 63
How to Hand Scissors or Knives to Someone You Like 65
If You Ever See My Soul Walking Down the Street 66
Thousandth Hill 67
What the Light Did Now 69
The Apricot Jelly Elegies 70
All The Folks Agree That This Is Terrible 72
Same Pajamas, but Everything Else Changes (Revision as
 Recurring Dream) 73
The Sound of Slowly Torn Up Grass for Grace 74
When I Heard *When I Heard the Learn'd Astronomer* 76
Tricycle 78
Last Six Hrs. of Summer 79
Did You Get My Email? 80
New Lang Syne 82
This Much 83

ACKNOWLEDGMENTS 85

A NOTE ABOUT THE AUTHOR 87

A NOTE ABOUT THE ANTHONY HECHT POETRY PRIZE 89

Foreword by Alice Fulton

The Goldfinch Caution Tapes. The title is almost a poem in itself. You can meditate on it like a koan as with many passages in this autumnal, darkly playful, deeply attentive book. In the title poem, caution tapes — those yellow and black plastic ribbons bordering sites of crime or upheaval — describe a bird's flight:

> … The goldfinch
> caution tapes light's shallow
> grave. I just came to watch it
> knock around in some trees
> but the lake explained every
> rain at once so here goes.

The excerpt contains threads that shimmer throughout the collection: Enclosure, lockdown. Seeing, perceiving. Rotational form. You have to circle and reread lines rich with syntactical ambiguity: The flying goldfinch is caution taping "light's shallow grave," the sunset and horizon. And the goldfinch caution tapes (are) light's shallow grave, a flight enveloping the darkening air. James D'Agostino is a mesmerizing juggler of semantics whose tactics sometimes seem akin to Emily Dickinson's adroit linguistic shifts. A poet of the new pastoral, ecopoetics, he offers no facile epiphanies. It is nature, the lake that explains as the light fades in rain, and "here," the sense of place, goes, dissolves.

Materiality is always going in this mind-bending collection. "You think these things / are bodies forever? You see / all the sky in that barn?" the title poem concludes. Here and not here, a relic of positive and negative space, the barn is a dematerializing ruin. The tone—exasperated, impatient—is characteristic, the casual diction of one who just came to watch the light "knock around in some trees," a speaker always on the lookout, keenly observing. The collection's tonal mixtape is acerbic, unstuffy, self-mocking—the opposite of pompous or officious.

The book's largest structure is rotational. The first poem is "Hello My Name," and the last ends "… Look, / I already told you. Hello." Another begins with the speaker recalling words he's researched:

Last Search

of mine you'll find *antidote*
and the one before that

anecdote. And before that's
asymptote, but we're getting

less and less ahead of
ourselves....

Antidote, anecdote, asymptote. Perhaps those terms can serve as arbitrary keys to the book's strategies. In "Hello My Name," D'Agostino turns fall, the elegiac season, into an antidote for elegy, a verb: "I like falling." We summer, we winter. But we fall is a first. It's one of the gentler moments in this sharply voiced collection as are these lines from "The Sound of Slowly Torn Up Grass for Grace:"

when hydrogen atoms
fuse into helium
in the furnace of
the sun, it can take
ten million years
to climb to the surface
and then it's nine
more minutes to us
down here where
luckily our aloes grow
mostly at the rate
we burn.

Two of the book's obsessions, time and measurement, exhibit a marvelous reciprocity as the sun helps aloes grow into an antidote to sun damage. "Mutually Assured Construction," a wildly delightful epithalamium, celebrates steadfast love as antidote to destruction.

> First two words they said to eachother
> were happy anniversary....
>
>   ... These two,
> they're a one-word each other. At first
> the typo's an accident, but you try keeping
> them apart.

And like the conversational meanderings of A. R. Ammons, D'Agostino's poems often are composed of anecdotal evidence gathered on rambles and road trips. His speaker is a roving intelligence, a pilgrim and traveler continually approaching a home away from home in the middle of midwest America, a muddle observed with piecemeal acuteness. Ammons's great ode, "The City Limits," seems a progenitor of D'Agostino's "Ardor Vitae," with its compressed rhythm and sublimely mundane collection of splitting and binding:

> For a long while, link a few little instants—staple
> stab, fender gleam, the simple aspiration of these weeds
> in window-colored wind or broken bottle held together
> by its label, only by its name in puddles rain zeroes
> and zeroes, then cloudbreak and blackbirds blued
> by sudden sun. The grasses roll. Lilacs brush the fence ...

Asymptote might be the most intriguing of the three terms. In projective geometry, an asymptote is a line tending toward infinity, approaching a given value or curve without ever quite meeting it. Lyric poetry is composed of lines that approach and intentionally fall short, implying without explaining, trusting the reader to get the meaning as one gets a joke. "Ever hear a light bulb cool?" the title poem asks, and it's a classic, real world example of asymptote—as well as a synesthesia that implodes the senses of sound and touch.

Like another mathematical conundrum, the Möbius strip, D'Agostino's brilliantly twisty work collapses the binaries of positive and negative space, inside and outside, first and last. There's a pervasive sense of lateness, afterness, overness. "Can I help whoever's last?" he asks in "Same Pajamas, but Everything Else Changes (Revision as Recurring Dream)." In "Tricycle" he writes "I already miss you / was how we met." And the eponymous poem "Listing" is dedicated to the German mathematician who first discovered the Möbius concept but published his findings after Möbius.

In addition to nonduality, a Möbius strip suggests entrapment. Language tries to trap what it names, but words fall short. When D'Agostino writes "… There / is nothing I'm not missing," you're forced to reorient yourself as one meaning is supplanted by another. It's a Möbius strip that works two ways: I'm missing—longing for—everything. And I'm missing—failing to see—everything ("Self-Portrait as Isaac Newton in Lockdown").

Lockdown and boundary are especially poignant tropes during years when a virulent virus required "social distancing" and the corona's spikey icon was everywhere:

> … where
> a close-up microbe screams from all our
> screens—risen hell nail face, muppet
> fiber art fever dream, many-bulbed
> edge of the Welcome to Las Vegas
> sign, where for one night only
> we're here all year.

("Gorilla by Jellyfish Light")

"Kindled Measures Going Out" considers the human tendency to inscribe everything with meaning. Flying swallows look like quotation marks, the hair on a soap bar says *ojos*. But D'Agostino sees all too well, as his tough self-appraisals testify. In "Play Attention" he tells those head-in-sand birds, "… hey / ostriches I could've been / what I am." Play attention, indeed. There's a whole lotta slippage going on, a tactic that replaces any steady perception with a vibrant doubleness. The title "I Am" puns on iamb and begins "Unstressed stressed isn't a poetic foot, it's a life / summary.…" And later: "… My dreams now are all just / violins and time travel. That's supposed to be / violence and timed travail.…" Wit is a weapon, an antidote to despair when "meaning it" is an act, a construct:

… Is it me? Is it us? Imagine

being miserable and armed with only earnest.
Since strangeness is a form of accuracy, shut up

and see, then act like you mean it.…

D'Agostino's poetry is inexhaustible in the most seductive way, and I say that with confidence after rereadings that left me boggled, dazzled, smitten, amazed, wowed, charmed. In the face of such, my remarks fall short, but D'Agostino offers this counsel:

… few people
get more interesting
the longer they speak
so get in the grave
of what you have
to say & get out baby …"

("Please Come")

Get in the groove that is "light's shallow grave." Though I can't adequately express the book's dissonant beauty, I can say it was thrilling to discover poems packed with infinite resonance that are infinitely fun to read. D'Agostino's mordant palimpsests, his contrary motions and emotions, wreaked sweet havoc in this reader's brain. Like the greatest lyric poetry, his poems kept—and keep—exceeding their bounds and creating revelation. What a surprise. What a find. What a cool poet. What a feast.

for Peter Carcia

Is there no way
to stop the houses falling
within the bird's body?

— Michiko Nogami

Hello My Name

The hammock
has no particular inhabitants
but sway. Autumnal

mums, evergreen dying
in splotches under
slowly bruising sugar

maples. Posers
without even holes
under their patches.

It's all news. It is
the wasp nest at the back
of the *Evening Star* box.

There's just one
squirrel. It flickers. Hello
my name is my face,

a holed-up sniper of joy.
I like it in a book
when there's a library.

I like falling.

You Are

This is the moment when lit
windows wonder the floor

and we try to write wander
but it comes out all light.

Autumn fields talcum each
other at dusk in stalk dust

come harvest, so whenever,
November. The late corn

outgrows its church clothes.
We don't have etherized

evening sky we've got
patients all night long.

Let us go then, you know,
us. Escape would be

a palindrome, if S's were
P's and the C disappeared.

If the sea disappears we've
been dead for years. For

the dew from the sweet grass
the dog licks her shins.

Your eyes aren't bloodshot
your blood just wants a look

for itself. It's not high-definition,
it's high-connotation.

Stars scooch an inch.
You're. It's that simple.

Spell it however you want.

40°N, 92°W

I'm going to try to be a person
one hoof at a time. I'm another guy
in a tie talking about light across
this county, too afraid of snakes
to handle anything, but love
love love any tongue spoken in.
In the graveyard on Neptune
Rd. our hound rolls on her back
on the frosted headstone shadow
grass, crunches and grunts, and
that's not buzzards chipping off
the airy blue, it's Neptutian leisure
gliders, which is what they are to us
terrestrials, too. Crawl all you
want our first steps are toward
the grave. Here's to getting lost.
Best case beauty ties your shoelaces
together. Worst it takes the foot.
My guess god's favorite part of earth's
thirty-some odd people in a church,
all a little bit off whisper mumbling
trespasses—the *ch* of its launch, plosive
blade in the belly, then all that July
Fourth sidewalk snake lit puck ash
extrusion hisses its slithered bed
of s's, i.e. Eden, and we're in.
A summer's worth of gardening
and peonies, I think, a week past
frost, black wrought-iron foliage in
a scribble at the base of a headstone.
Mid-Nov, about three inches into
that tangle, a little bit still lives.
It's the last of the yet to freeze
pale green, nesting deep enough
in its dead leaf shield to terraform
a few days more, to drip the last

few photons of its fading signal
over our horizon. Hey. What's
Hal finally say in *2001*? I can
feel it. I can feel it.

Please Come

— after Vallejo

I will die
in like five seconds
here in this
marsupial pouch
of Missouri summer
if I have to listen
to myself talk
about death again
I will die & I'm not

going to lie
there's a lesson in this
few people
get more interesting
the longer they speak
so get in the grave
of what you have
to say & get out baby
you don't have to
shout it

can be just one
word whispered
nests
written in the trees
avian lice & mites
this city its lights
in mud & spit
& woven twigs
birds swirl
their single vowel O

fringed flyers
bottom feeders
of the heavens O

wet black eye
bead please come
daybreak blink
the bright world
back

Prairie Warble

Overlook the river from far enough
away you first mistake the lit-up theater
lot for water, when it would take its asphalt
real recent rain to mirror polish purple
dusk like that—through blue ash to hurt
pink cuticle of horizon where the photo
rips in two from a pretty true tear
of treeline. America's got trouble
with its key card so the weekend worker
puts her bag and coffee, lunch and folders
down to re-swipe and re-swipe until it
looks like she's touching up the *A*
in *Fuck America* tagged onto the face
of the Natural History Museum. It's
only natural, though, if history lets you
out. From inside the old state capitol,
the *BLM* spray-painted on the window
must look in reverse like *ML8* which
if you say it enough starts to sound out
immolate if it wants to, and *homily* if it
must. Even the Streets and San sidewalk
repair notation spray-paints specks
into the epic. All those half hashtags
on certain sections of cement to save
leave us enough F's to fuck the cops,
find consonants in pavement cracks,
and read the real duet of our disrepair,
from our storm drains now loud
vowels.

Last Sunday of Summer

We're a part of this harvest
moon never mind the cloud
cover. That cardinal clinking
coins. I'm always three pages
away, troubled, but with
measurables. Walnut thumps
come between smaller
and smaller slices of silence.
Lately it's not light and dark,
it's light and lit, whole shadows
of it, even though today
the drear reared word-ward,
drew weird birds. That's no way
to write's the way to, too.
I mean you buy it, you break it.
Had a kid in my office tell me
he's been told he's romantic
lead or shark of a lawyer,
so I gave him Anne Carson
only until Thursday. Another
one told me he couldn't take
anything out of his poem
because he's already lost so
much, so I told him come back
later for Anne Carson. Who'd
say to a sunrise I know skies
who do what you do only way
way better? Pierce the crepe
of experience and out gurgles
nice ripe nectarine light,
well, it might. Poet, go on
the g, not on the o.

—for Dean Young 1955-2022

Last Search

of mine you'll find *antidote*
and the one before that

anecdote. And before that's
asymptote, but we're getting

less and less ahead of
ourselves. I remember

the reflection of TV light
on your teeth. I'm trying

to sing but it's coming out
gibberish, try speaking

in tongues and out
comes elocution. Again

the troposphere goes slow
coals and the window's

last glimpse of it turns
out to be neon *gyros* glow,

and you go no though
even as you say it know

it's pretty much yeah.
You can only get this

far out of your head—
pinhole stereoptic clouds

in the sky of your skull.
Belly / wing coloring

blinks sand to sea / sand
to sea on a swallow, but deer

is where god held the sky
when she painted it sunset.

Quantum Tantrum

At one point in development
Pac-Man was Chompsky.
The week I was born
the number one song

was Send in the Clowns.
End of Feb the first half
inch of daffodils don't defile
a thing. They say we are

twenty days ahead toward
Spring which almost gets us
whole. We're three weeks
late with everything, but

whatever little purple vents
the violets opened in the earth
must've done their work
b/c one dove on the phone

line blows its pop bottle
vowel and just like that
we're all still here. A mile-off
vulture slow scoots its cone

of carrion scan and I could
care less more often which
is just boredom and a big
problem. Bigger still there

might not be a single poem
in it, but the job's work
the spine of the notebook,
strengthen your core. Pry,

encrypted ear, a prayer.
Day goon, yon god dog,
do agony. Nod and go
your life is any good yo.

Evolutionary Aesthetic Safeguard

Tonight the moon's a cut
round of rock sausage hung

in a rope in the butcher shop
window of the cosmos.

Moon's got a lot of mouth
to feed, of work to do. Life

ate my lunch lettuce. So what?
What am I going to do?

I'm going to open-face
the day. I'm going to spend

less time in those impromptu
press conferences of the mind.

First of all, let me just say
to my creator, ouch. I mean

Momma. The cowlick's how
I like it.

Attack Decay Sustain Release

Two small towns rub their mail
all over each other at the speed
of reading, the speed of walking,
really. Feel it? Spring just now

something. The white lilac throws
up Satan's fingers. Whatever died
around here's going to start to stink.
Even traffic splash past pavement

far enough away's a wave. It's spring,
we'd like to do a few great things even
if it means breaking. Buds herniate
even further. I am bio-degradation.

I'm trying to write a song called
Spring, but mostly I'm just home
hiding. I've got a few layers of self
to burn off before I can even begin

to see robins beak up worms that
you can tell (by the way the bird
whips its whole head up and
back and really leans into it)

don't want to go.

Out Into the Worldness I Did Roam

In the real America I keep slowly breathing
shallow, wait to gulp the perfect mix of dead
skunk and distance. I'm trying to get to the edge
of the sky but it did or it does last bubbles in
flat cola. Plenty of fog to prove who I was.
Rain is something's biting zeroes on the lake.
The game is didn't want to look but heard
the flies anyway. Round here ain't going
nowhere so maybe every landscape's a portrait
in reverse where those roads got pretty after
you left and none of you lives on or otherwise
stencils out shadows. We were born to smell
extinguished candles, the cake's just gravy.
Cool wet spring hot dry summer molds
the corn so harvest plumes black dust up
behind the combines. An apricot moth pair
sutures cartoon air. I walk and I read and
spend time in the trees. I'm trying to remember
whether I do not think that they will sing for
me or don't think they will sing *to* me. Dawn
pinched its skin in the day / night hinge again,
pools a little blood on the horizon. What I will
miss about having a skull's how quick dreams
respond to stimuli, the alarm goes off and it's
someone with your stolen guitar somewhere
in the parking garage carnival dead letter office
of your life and you've got to get it back, there
in your galoshes as everyone still watches
the dream dream back at you who
grabs my shoulder, says it's late.

—Daniel Johnston 1961-2019

The Goldfinch Caution Tapes

Second full day of autumn
we've got another shot to
get summer in the ground
before anyone starts asking
around. Without a director
of field studies it's up to us
to slink the webs with rain
drops, to blue jay nail gun
three quick calls, to stand
under your sky and count
the ribs in the umbrella.
In the wet campfire ash
clasped shut the moth's
just cinder, but sprung
tripwire flying's pure blue
sky. You're rooting for
the world. Like a dog. You're
like a dog. The goldfinch
caution tapes light's shallow
grave. I just came to watch it
knock around in some trees
but the lake explained every
rain at once so here goes.
If it feels your life is in pieces
why aren't your poetries, you
little library, you little liars?
You know you don't have
an elm, you got hackberry at
best. Maples off their meds
dye half their heads, look
slept in. It's something
everyone in universe sees.
Just not me. I'm not afraid
of ghosts. I'm afraid ghost
is best a lateral move.
Ever hear a light bulb cool?

Talk into a drained pool?
You think these things
are bodies forever? You see
all the sky in that barn?

Kindled Measures Going Out

Swallow flock floats
its quotation cloud above
the tall corn. The hair

on my soap says *ojo*.
Look. If you believed
a beam lighthoused

out from the eye and
its sweep through things
was seeing, you'd be

Heraclitus. Toadstools
in a pasture rise in
a pattern of parentheses.

End of August fog blue
gauze on the bean field.
Go ahead. Step in

all you want doesn't
make it a river.

Besos de los Perros

In monotonous,
the o's go 2, 4, 6, 8,

and who do we appreciate?
Whom? All pattern
is investment in future
violation. You are

someone with one idea
until you screw it up
and then you got two,
too. It's a fission
of just fucking around.
It's the quickest pot

to boil, the one you don't
know what to do with.
Maybe you unwrap
the lettered bankrolls
of work to let the wrists
breathe. Maybe you
unwrap the lettered
bandages of words to

let the wounds a little
while. Duh, we were

luminous. We were dark
wires in glass bulbs. We
were screwed. We had one
about trees, but we had

a lot of ideas. Today is
day-to-day. The sun
an orange syringe and
side effects are not

shutting up and shadows.
The sunflower row goes
scorched headache end
of August. I go garbage
to garbage to write stuff
like that on the way
to school, each can's
closed lid a desk,
a spot to set my coffee,
open my notebook

and go: I loved every
classmate who ever

collected my homework
when I was out sick,
but can't recall ever
doing any of it.

I remember chapter
numbers, study questions,
stacks that made no sense,
but stood as sweet little
totems from the world
gone on without me.

The little Milky Way
of millet constellating
in the toast. At most
the reader's only every
poem you've read that
week. Out here we are
on our own, but we're
in this together.

This Foolishness About Moons and Blossoms

It's good to have something
that's interesting you're bad at.
I mean the emotion's available,
it's just a distribution problem.
The nut trees buy up gold off
late night local tv ad scares.
You come here not to punch
the clock but to punch it.
Backlit milkweed's part
medieval weapon, part pillow
fight, so it's just like life,
which comes down to what's
wrong with me / what's wrong
without me. You're not talking
to an imaginary therapist you
can't afford, you're bored.
Pineapple juice light, apple
cider light, clipped to the
trees by bird beak, leaf by
life. The wind and those oaks
are fine on their own, but
when they sit together
not only distract each other,
they distract everyone around
them. Later when the night
air reactivates the scent of
soup from your face, you'll
sit in the mist to pinpoint
rain's very moment of
conception, but the language
of the fuck up's fucked up.
You can't get an urge in
wedge-wise. See? Teeth
that want to cut go herringbone
but teeth that want to sing
are all lined up. The game is

keep the shovelful of dirt
out of your mouth. Go into
moment control. Click enter.
Double click enter.

Bomb Threat Near the Library of Congress

white bored white board
writes what

terms conditions what he
wants at least

until a remote tactical robot
wobbles up with its dedicated

phone line to negotiate
and if that won't work plan

b's deploy Amanda Gorman again
in floor-length canary cold hope

of January down the stairs and up
to his toy truck to tell him what

step out into this wonderous this
gold-limbed simply unfinshed

afternoon step out
into somehow what we have

weathered a sea we

step into

Dear Amanda

Our fourth wave froths forth, WTF.

My dog walks under a tent of web she leash-shears from its anchor strand and it slow furls there in mere air dozes

lit jellyfish flounce of Sunday morning light which might be my tithe. Today I don't believe in.

God though. Know her name makes tons possible. And pain.

I ♥ Amanda painted backwards on a bedroom window in a place abandoned for years that up-north elbow-break in Main St. Torn out vines pock the siding.

Something pulled that hard to stay.

Sitting on the stoop that last mailbox nail means more to the porch beams than it ought but who am I? To say a fall-apart porch owes each of its splinters a goddamn thing I wouldn't.

On this no big deal bed of nails your pillow's a bag of hammers and your sleepy head's no better for my lullaby.

Sage brush bunch grass miffed affection. I am just trying to know something small about us all. At home I open up my mirror. I spray deodorant on clothes like I'm not even here.

The theme of my prom was Somebody.

Shoelace dog leash quads and calves—how can I prolong my passing 215 N. Main and each trip pocket some pebble from its beach.

Those drop biscuit butter-topped clouds make all this late afternoon pink: rose jam.

All curtains have spiders. We all want to eat the light. Or eat to light the want whatever.

Each day I want to put a letter in the mailbox hung face down mouth open that falls right out. You want to meet someone from a faraway place go home.

I'm chewing my teeth to the dust I'm just behind them.

There's no way I'm not catching this thing. I need a good thermometer and a crate of all I'll call crawlables and go no further now. Maybe ground glass lungful's how our past reassembles cathedrals.

Or I love you's a painter and Amanda's Amanda.

The porch creak pip squeak's a scorched creep who only once peeps and the neighbor's oblivious and oblivion's a living room and obviously I'm not Amanda I ♥ Amanda I'm her

neighborhood's nocturnal blur. We only deserve a couple of us. Two beauty bushes back to school bloom and shed petals eye shadow the lawn.

Monday is a vector and Tues worse than expected. A line of text half hidden in the scroll ascenders look like a far-off skyline nearing Indy maybe Tulsa.

The dead all barf up dust over the sides of their little wooden dinghies that's life. That's what a sleepy plea pays poesy for here athwart the yawp slope, oh, we hear ye we're just not locking on.

We're not where we were, where we wear away—year, era—timeline this long you've got to skip it like a stone to get across because this bottle's not empty yet so any note's on hold but it won't be long before

I await your reply.

Listing

—for Johann Benedict Listing, the unacknowledged other discoverer of the Mobius strip

what was on it. He smoothed the crushed
                                        paper and read

                              *

              this fallen tree's hull is the sentence. The mites' eaten trail in

                              *

        mountain by mountain
        for hours. The rain arriving
                                  erases the range

                              *

in fact changes any thesis. The way
                              dropping to your knees

                              *

        advances and retreats. Take these
                                        dispatches about

                              *

massive trade in breakables. A preponderance
                              of shards implies

*

        the world
                is to want to save it. One response to

*

skies they're falling from. Attitude
                        also means the way planes are in

*

        eyes they resemble. Then you're picking olives
                                because of whose

*

    one long leaving. The river in its living glaze is

*

was and would be all along. The thing it was
                            back then was

*

to be a plum blossom
is a little blood
in balled-up cellophane.

Trash spills across the lawn
until what appears

Self-Portrait as Isaac Newton in Lockdown

Forget *standing on the shoulders*
of giants, it's scaling the shins
alone should be a life's work.

Coffee rings read early diagrams
of eyes, Newton's, who worked
a metal rod *betwixt my eye &*

the bone as neare to the Backside
as I could to note the colors when
he pressed a nerve. What do you

expect? He left London to wait
out the plague at a family farm,
and poking around in there

from the center saw greene, blew,
purple, darke purple, blew, greene,
yellow, red like flame, yellow, greene,

blew, broade purple, darke. Pinhole
projectionist, why am I always
looking at the same things to say?

Gas can, roof fan, cloud wrung
spear light plastic bags snag.
It's just jigsaw's all it is. Violets

zombie angels up through clumps
of dead leaves, which must make
a perfect greenhouse top to cook

and coax them out now. Time
of year every bird's got something
in its mouth, some grub, some

plug of mulch to nest with, song
to stake some claim, because song
is what belongs to you. It tents up

territory. Phone lines lute string
this big empty chamber. There
is nothing I'm not missing.

Wake

"The body goes down to the ground alone."
— John Blumer, gravedigger, New Montefiore Cemetery, Long Island, NY

If the difference between the 20th
and 19th century is the difference

between the words *cemetery* and *graveyard*,
then the difference between the 21st

and 20th is the front-page photo
of those big cardboard boxes printed *head*

at one end, and the word *casket*. Let me
begin with a bath because it's not even

6 and I've seen a gallery of pics
of body bags and footage of a drone

flown over grave diggers filling a trench
of unclaimed named, and now I need to fold

myself up, still warm, open the window,
see the steam rise from my chest and vanish.

Good Morning Night

Two weeks away from a time change
we lose an hour and call it spring, drop

an eon it's a rounding error. The news
today is all Neanderthal Wall Art!

and we're like warlocks? whoa, no,
64 thousand years ago someone with

a pronounced brow did this, made these
cave paintings. The paper called it

a ladder structure, but I bet it's a bed.
And someone done in red's getting

into it or out. My phone's thin skin
of cave wall palm glow allows me in

to zoom around. Pachyderm dermis
relief map topographic sea floor plan

lunar surface in the millennial mineral
trickle. Two stalactites to the right

the horse waits facing away or it could
be someone's legs you're lying next to

looking down on, moony head resting
on your shoulder, talking about the past.

1847

A town so small
it had two names.
Lower Iron Bridge

and Lindenville.
It is not the end.
It's Highway N.

It's the way in
through autumn
hills one great big

blood blister,
the gravel road
a single strand

of au pair hair
woven in the
comb's dark loom

of the family.
Summer snares
the sawmill

in a lasso of yellow
wildflower so
the P.O. renamed it

Yarrow. East side
grist mill, west side
bar. Originally built

in 1847, destroyed
by ice floes in 1847.
They could have

1847

named it Comeback.
They could have
never left.

American Gothic

Once I read the headline *Iowa Town Will Vote to Disappear* I knew right then all these years I'm mayor. Hadn't heard how the final count turned out. Didn't think I would. Knew parking wasn't a problem. Power and light now come from the county. The sheriff's still the shit. Smoke up out of the tall corn untwists its braid of blackbirds. Skunk blood ink spill dabbed at with a paw piece keeps the scavengers in meat. In this heat buzzards lift black murk up to heaven, and bring a little more hunger back down to keep us awake at the wheel. That's the deal. I'm halfway away from either of us. 80 mi. outside Iowa City, 80 more to my door in Missouri. You're kinda not any where, you're kinda not everywhere's the problem with living apart, a two-home no one, your living in parts. You're living in parts. Beanfield to the left, corn on the right's like walking with one shoe. An acre up it flips, so the limp shifts, tilts the tall slosh of sun across this road where up ahead someone pulls off into shade with a flatbed filled three melons deep. Hills Bros. can left out for the dollar, so we're on our honor here in Fairfield or whatever comes after it, little town called Amends.

Derek Chauvin

— not for Derek Chauvin

There's only one name to say in this
and it's not his, one knee to close
the airway with, a hand to fill the pocket
and the knee to shut out shouts, the artery,

the avenues. That hand was what white
performance of this dominion I'm in on?
The cop's vile idle walk in the park posture
(at ease officer as you were carry on).

The hand in the dark in there grasps
what? That you're the one to hold this
world together? Zip-tie by zip-tie? Why lie
that hand was for the live stream,

poised, a pose, a poison. We're all in
enough of this snuff film now.
We're the key grip and we're losing it,
this series a slur so the franchise only

ever ends with a prequel, with a trailer,
with concessions, with a ticket to cloud
blue crowd source serial murder. Late May
light in the administrative leaves. Wait

who's in shorts, shit that's his shoulder. There
is no whole. And no one letter added later
makes it so, only this hole to fall sick in
the scroll of the old corrosive, the immobile

torso. Your name is what the welts spell.
It's not not my hell, not yet, but it's on
my mind. It's in the spine trying to stand
in the street, in the sun, this form, a foam,

Derek Chauvin

the name a stain, a caustic acrostic, and I
won't stack it like that, I still won't say.
Each day, each ache, an acrid chain
hacked into evidence. Evince and hear

a heaven, have a cure, inch ever nearer,
a thousand years til overhead at last
the sounds of trowels
scratch in light.

Wiping My Ass with Your Kiss

-print excess lipstick tissue I took
from our bathroom trash can good bye
is all I can do today it's all I can say

how afraid to face my lungs already
lace on x-ray screens in dreams. Fuck

your MTWRF what day of the dead
is it? It's 60K and not even breakfast
yet. Not nearly enough late April leaf

to keep the vulture shadow from
slicing bud branch trunk clean through

to the mud under us all. But this
biohazard's my own blather, invisibly
after me like daylight astrology. Fate

shiv-sticks star-pricks in the throat
of the cosmos and at most it's creek

mist, not creation myth, at most it
goes: those white blooms I thought
to bring you, reached to, were bird

shit splattered leaves of weeds. I don't
have the adhesive to hold it together

yet. Two dead trees fallen into each
other squeak in the wind like a kiss,
and how's it not one, just with no

lips? Or in the parlance of our virus
if you die I'll fucking kill you.

Gorilla by Jellyfish Light

Baby elephant trunk-bumps the beluga
pod, and two months in I figure out why
I like animals touring empty zoos.
In desolation porn the world goes on
without our fingerprints all over it—
the best parts of us, wonder and awe,
if unsteady on glossy terrazzo.
On our handler's social media
we're only so free. Just because I am
also alive but still a dick, I pantomime
a coughing fit, walking the dog to get
someone up ahead to switch sides
of our street. I'm sorry. I'm worried
someone else's handwriting's going to
finish this, yours or a coroner's, in dates
and times and temperatures until, *2 inside,*
in spray paint on our door. The world
inside's all eyelid light fixture just stucco
dreaming, under which we are each other's
essential worker. We're one another's
wet market, open for biz, with a taste
for something. Carnivorous coronavirus,
scour in vain for us via cursor, where
a close-up microbe screams from all our
screens—risen hell nail face, muppet
fiber art fever dream, many-bulbed
edge of the Welcome to Las Vegas
sign, where for one night only
we're here all year.

The Liberal Arts

When you're not looking for any particular
tool each rock you find's perfect for something

but what? Wednesday wind storm early enough
into autumn not to bring a lot of leaves down.

Summer's weld held and here we are in the violent
shade, thrashing and thrashing at light, and I'd

hazard where the sun comes up by the .02
suture-thread-thin moon that can't keep all

the bleeding in so here's your morning held over
for observation. You're okay. You just don't know

how to not know anything yet. Pretty soon
light's so sharp it hits this little beach flush,

each rock's got a dark side, each is an eclipse,
this bone chip guitar pick, one stone face

of my father, one wet chunk of heart wall.
When I get this winded I get weepy. It's just

me and the vultures—two today, and me, wait,
three. I didn't have anything to say I didn't

find along the way. You know how home
I'm going? The vultures sail higher. Either

I'm a liar or alive.

Eureka

The plan was an elixir for eternal life
but kaboom came gunpowder. The plan
was cure the migraine, but the by-product

was Coke. The plan was shag the pigeons
from the arms of the antenna. Once done
the hiss that's left is big bang background

static. Now you've done it. You've held
an upturned cup to the bedroom door
of God, as he bumps around inside, up

to older brother stuff. My plan was pick
my classes and get the hell back home,
but this cute short-haired girl from Boston

wouldn't shut up. Just like the birth of
the universe, my Tuesday Thursday was
physics, chemistry, biology, but my

Monday Wednesday spooled it all up
in reverse: modern, early modern,
medieval, ancient, and just like that,

we're back at the start. Coyote with
a bladderful of ocean, a coatful of burrs
the stars were bound to be. We're less

than terrestrial. Any constellation is
a tattoo on time. We've been splitting
atoms for years, but can't put shit back

together. Technically, you are only really
responsible for falling, but gravity's
the weakest force, so your job's to get

back up. Yesterday someone told me
about an alarm clock that won't stop
until your feet hit the snooze mat on

the floor. Intention must be thwarted,
according to Matisse, as one prunes
trees. But who expected death?

The plan was to be born. If you want
to hear God plan,
laugh.

Mutually Assured Construction

—for J and C

First two words they said to eachother
were happy anniversary. Third was jinx.
Sometimes the best thing to remember
about a word is how to misspell it. Half

that tree sways in the breeze, half don't
know that dance, but it's okay. Down here
between the isobars, no ghosts were harmed
in the making of these bodies. These two,

they're a one-word *each other*. At first
the typo's an accident, but you try keeping
them apart. Once the sugars collect and
catch, it's unstoppably autumn. It's Fall

in Love Day, two-for-one and one for
both. It's goldleaf on the tongue and a whole
lot of song left to go, but we're coming to
the chorus now. If anyone among us

objects to this union, we wouldn't even
trust you with cake, with a spoon. From this
day on, late in any early October water
will try to go everywhere the wind talks it

into. Fireflies can't get off the grass, just
like the bridal party or cities seen from
space. Sugars trapped on clear days, cool
nights purple the reds and age the gold.

So begins the end of the beginning
of autumn; tomorrow you wake to start
its heart. Feel that? Some flip switched,
so right now you don't even have time

for haiku. Nut trees go old gold / early
then wait out fall's / reddened whenever. /
We forget summer's / just lots of sticks
underneath / all its windy skins. We've

got a little less than eleven and a half hours
of daylight today and I've already talked
away this much of it. Another hour or two
and dusk might do blackberry buckle,

the candle spit out shadows. If people can
make time for craft beer they can make
time for craft emotion. It's so much easier
to hold it together when you sorta smash it

between eachother. To get better together,
tether, and remember: I don't need
a thing / from you but to sit there
and / tell me what you want.

With the Crew

Everyone remembers
the alien hatching

through the breastplate
of the astronaut, but no

one knows how I feel
right now, and I don't

either, don't know if
I remembered to close

the hatch or not, if I
levelled with the crew

yet, etc. It could be
anybody's birthday.

My favorite frosting's
the picture.

Play Attention

Early autumn some dozen
drops into its first rain.

Leaves exhale terpene
and isoprenoids as they die,

but all fall walnuts also
toss off golden eyelids.

Cold mist just sits up and
drifts on this little lake,

which found its 286th
way to draw sky this year

alone. This year's alone
and the lake's just a lens

on a hole this whole Oct
hour last clouds do loose

coals. The belief's real but
the god's just phosphorous,

his petrichor preposterous.
It's not I'm not buying it

it's we aren't even in the store
yet. At this point it would

take hardly anything to ruin
my day. I'll turn an aisle

see a bunch of soup cans
stacked in columns and say hey

ostriches I could've been
what I am.

I Am

Unstressed stressed isn't a poetic foot, it's a life
summary. You hoofed it to the cold sunset

just to watch something pretty die, aside from
America. This early in the year, that high

in the sky Orion's bound to be a spinal when
he finally faceplants. My dreams now are all just

violins and time travel. That's supposed to be
violence and timed travail. But it only takes

a minute marveling the flock to lock onto the one
with the limp. Pity's pretty simple. I would call

a mental health day, but I am basically brainstem
with a good bibliography. I go cave door, foyer,

space hatch, tether tube, umbilicalled imbecile
tumbling—foresight, hindsight, insight—pissing

orbital bones into the skull of the snow. I am
as funky as the next guy, but don't know why

we need that much bassline in our pharmaceutical
ad disclaimer bed. Is it me? Is it us? Imagine

being miserable and armed with only earnest.
Since strangeness is a form of accuracy, shut up

and see, then act like you mean it. On the just-
started half-hearted fence, new snow falling.

It's still New Year's. Any key on your ring
you don't know the door for, forget.

Iron-Clad Lullaby

I've often tried to figure out why,
without looking it up
because that would be too easy,
the world is not a book.
Rain in sheets, itself
an ink, all squall
until instantly it stills,
steams in the street
once the sun
picks back up where it
last left off. Just north
of Bachelor, exit 155
leads east to the Missouri Girls Town
and west toward Nostalgiaville.
So again life's laid right out
with a highway down its spine,
making this 2-way stop its middle
age, and Nostalgia, an algae
occluding ponds some are fond of
finding time to skate on and later
remember about 85% of,
so more and more clouds
are pressed into absent mountain
service, and that
stands in for this,
the way cotton blown
across the road makes due
with Michigan winters
merely remembered.

How Not to Float Off Into Space

If you're not down here
tangled in the names of things
sit very still. Only look at
what makes you notice. Once
it's low enough to ripple over
pebbles, the creek face gets
a rib cage, and even a cursory
review of extant lit swears
a heart's not far behind.
What a find, might not match
JR's arrowheads and blow dart
bone, but still I'm silt-soaked,
still got all bit up, climbed
back out with this orange
jewel weed. Good days
you go for your phone and
it's not there so you pat
your pocket, now your body's
got to be the camera, and that
blink right there's your shutter
speed, and there—what a body
of work!—luckily a film of silver
lines the inside of your skull
so the pluses blooming further
into asterisks on the vine stay
little Phillips heads that leave
a lot of nicks in the photo plate
named sweet autumn clematis,
the one we're all trapped in
again, trying to make room,
ballooning over tombs.

Culled from the Lull

I usually don't like to look at the dailies
but lately can't look away. In the rafters
of the park shelter shiver little birds in
beds of mud. Already Karen's at the studio
making hanging cloud, the Japanese paper
saved for printing poems. It's a privilege
to have nothing to say. Even the bird shit
on this picnic table imprints its little yin
yang symbols, chiaroscuros our chances
as not half bad or good, but both. It's not
Zen, but it's too late to start for real, so
what? It's September in our immediate
surroundings and we're immediately
surrounded. Barbed wire sine wave wet
morning light. A spider's lit thumbprint
web rippling liquid in a little wind. Our
solar system drifts through the local
interstellar cloud, also called the Local
Fluff, while down here cottonwoods slo
mo single feather pillow fight. Down
here sea slosh slows the spin of the globe,
so we've got one extra second yet
of summer to squander. They say we've
got ten miles of visibility today, but I bet
we won't use most of it. See? That little
sunlit knot of gnats, a vortex cloud of
fuck or feed, a form. Or clover over
graveyard grass, the pom pom squad
of the dead. That sundress strap of street
up the narrow shoulders of these hills.
See? Reduced cognitive filtering won't
help you learn Excel, but might make you
make something out of some of this.
Kicked-out window corner black cat
facsimile. Crown rack of cloud. Uptown
fountain water falling down onto itself

slaps back with the sound of a butcher
wrapping bloody chops in brown paper
or someone coming up toward us
through late autumn leaves for a word.

Headlit owl snake in its claws lifts
just enough off the still-hot highway
to clear my car. It's an Aztec instant
pictogram. It's one second of struggle
in the dark, maybe a minute more
depending where the nest is and how
hungry the owlets are. That's a pretty
tough group of back-up singers. Dark
Night and the Owlets. Skinned Snake
and the Owlets doing "Wet Pink Writhe,"
doing "Rope of Trouble Tying You to Me
(Without You)." And all the songs end
the same. Repeat to fade, which I hate
to love, but I'll live on as a coffee-
sheened thumbprint on some barely
returned library book. Even now I can
feel the whole history of its recall and
damage descriptions. The great books
ride a river of really late fees all the way
into the green sea of your eyes, so
obviously mud and leaf and cried out
cola. I'm glad for all this gloom this
morning and not the last so we could see
a little of the lunar eclipse. Today is just
the foam backing of the newest carpet
of sky and we're the hard luck wood
floor it hides. Let's start the socks-on
dance off now. Let's wade a while
the wavelength change. The winner
of the dance competition is the first
to know she's in one. The winner of
the marriage is the second one to stay.

The Past Grows Steadily Around One ...

> like a placenta for dying.
> —John Berger

One and a half rooms into
our lives, the robot vacuum
was born our child, our dirt

in its smile. We'd sleep to it
sing. We sometimes hid and
sought. Sometimes sent it

back to dock in the dark.
One dream torn up
into waking that summer

was whatever we've lost
on Mars, probably fueled
by news from our radio

alarm that NASA's scaling
back its search for Spirit,
the rover that failed to wake

from winter hibernation.
I just knew it was a little
box beeping in the dust.

I knew it knew. I loved
how every story about it
for a while used the word

crevasse. I even love how
I used to love you less
than I do now somehow.

In the morning we got
what we wanted. The place
seems clean.

Ardor Vitae

For a long while, link a few littler instants—staple
stab, fender gleam, the simple aspiration of these weeds
in window-colored wind or broken bottle held together
by its label, only by its name in puddles rain zeroes
and zeroes, then cloudbreak and blackbirds blued
by sudden sun. The grasses roll. Lilacs brush the fence
barbs and lilies star a yard, little help with wind
the blades wave onward and along, but then it's still,
and the trees just plants. The trees ring. I'd be fine
with each year's end of summer suffering
us such suffix, if only I knew then what we knew
then. The sky a marble rye a few birds fly, a kind
of caraway, though let's not get carried away
with this vision's pigeons, letter-legged, I beg you.
In wind these leaves aren't the tethered feathers
of held back birds, but another world squinted into,
another rouse to true, screw to loosen, hurt worth
a sermon, surely, but what about the mirth of mumblers
under their umbrellas? So Summer stumbles into what
it is, what it's going to have to have been. We came to
the end and kept on middling. This is how it works.
The well-worn thoughts knot and scram, lump up
then evaporate. I therefore think I am, and follow
the fish-shaped shadows of the almond-shaped
leaves of these walnut trees under which we wonder
what to just do. Clouds school. The sky's blue spools.
And that'll do a while. A couple of cumulonimbus
do their humble crumble, at least stood for something.
Anything. Falling, even. Down. Into this gristle
and its bone, this little book of knitted throws,
of antique barbs in which it's not too late,
its Dodge Six Point Stars and Knickerbockers,
the Kelly Thorny Common, the Four Point Twirl
on Large Strands, Twirl on Small, and on and on
along the fenced up wiry skies which wash this grit
of stars.

Among the Attributes of a Basically Cruel Man

Today began a dreamsicle
made of dirt and up to us
to pilot this sky's specific
dye lot. And why not?

Our lives are six or seven
people a lot, a couple dozen
less so, and an even call it
hundred lesser still. Today

it's the cinnamon blush
of rust on a dumpster.
It's the city's talc of salt
and still ice bites onto the lot

in a couple spots. Took the skull
for a crawl is all and tried not to
fall through a city ultimately
solveable, mere matter

of form. The locksmith's truck
fits surely into traffic. I've
climbed through four windows
twelve times, emerged smudged

or scraped, but home, where
the thing about charm's it
doesn't give a fuck what
comes after adoration, only

more and more.

Immediately Dismissed from the Accident

Let's ditch this benchmark
in an oratory shake-up. Let's
close our fabrications and just
pigpen it. Close your eyes and
picture it: tall enough an oak
so the top leaves fringe out
into fennel. Look, we really
better get back to trouble,
to watching Allen Ginsburg
turn another *grubber* into
a *courage-teacher*. To what
outcome? Which curriculum
kicks Lang Arts in its rickety
plums? This rhyme's a skin
that keeps its person in, but
the membrane gives both ways,
so the world swirls inside and
the body goes bye bye, but just
for a while. Is that the Hubble
telescope? No, it's the history
of our sneezes. Can't we count
our ice broken now? Here in
this trash cache we can't, we
just can't be held reprehensible.
We're all unglued sobs, shipping
consent and empirical research
into what's even syllableable
at all. It's OK just sound it out.
A4 and B3 are the only things we
can afford in this vending machine
of clouds, but what are we in
the moon for in the first place?
To re-skin this sycamore graft
by graft? Even with nothing
to say we've still a beautiful
silhouette to watermark.

How to Hand Scissors or Knives to Someone You Like

First write the treatise on the causes of the giving
way of walls, then, separately,

                                treat their remedies. Let the uncut

        mood
clutter up. Let the let down now

                               let down their guard again. Go
                ahead.
Grind your teeth
away each night then wake first thing to sing, sunlight
a local solvent of years, and yet

                            each day, each minute in it
the old song crumples newly, smoothes
to prose that holds up mirrored

                      sunglasses to nature, out there

where the hibiscus twists its photographs of flowers,
where we laughed best
and last and made the most of the mint, cups of snow
with our Kaluha.

                Write night stood
opposite, the only prop. Write how it next subsides
in greater collapse, then how it comes to topple.

                                  Then why.

Trouble deepened,
                yet made it safe enough for finally diving
into what the dearest to him persist in
calling my life, the long deep

clear I steered
of everyone. Clouds straight face

                      this horizon that wants to bring
              them all in anyway

for a few routine questions. It's not the name in the airport p.a.

but that someone somewhere's calling.

If You Ever See My Soul Walking Down the Street
You Better Cross to the Other Side of Heaven

Motherfucker, I love you,
and am sorry about screaming that
at you in the dream
which buck-knifed me awake
this morning. No, night hadn't
even started sweeping up,
tipping the seats of the chairs
onto tables as image
of where all these meals end
up if we're lucky, the place
setting to the seat to the simile,
pressed into a kiss like
whichever cube of kid's
cute scared face your school
yearbook photo closed to.
Mine met there in the dark
a picture of an early-stage
homecoming float chicken
wire-framed mustang, and
once our class long kiss
tongue spits with wild horses
in the dark that young we see
I don't know different things
in the campfire coals, so
one cold dark morning
years later we go for a walk,
we who want to apologize for
our dreams. Have mercy on us.
We're wide awake.

Thousandth Hill

        Stems that long
no wonder it's forever

to the reservoir
            at that lope of yours,

            cloud-colored crane.
I don't know why

they moved the swim line
            out after the drowning.

            It could've been drift.
Could've been disturbed

by the dredge. Everything
            at the shore starts

            looking like a shell. If it
holds still I'd held it

to my ear. Harvest sky
            gets back six odd feet

            of cornstalk, but hectarage,
acreage, field on field

on field, and you're pretty
            soon talking about real

            darkenss. A dz. buzzards
slow loom a Tues. coasting

through the next to last Sept.
            blue afternoon. Leave me

a little shin skin, Lord,
I might want to wade.

What the Light Did Now

In the graveyard whitetail deer wave
kerchiefs of old gravedigger ghosts
and get away again. Life, butt out.

They call it Bloomfield but right now
out there the stubble's staring into you
too, does the old you get a haircut joke

no I had my ears lowered. Good thing
too the sky's about to burst. It's used
up all its cloud space now has to pay

$2.99 to upgrade or let all this wet light
waste. I'm in the arts I mean an asshole
broke clown. I keep this ugly chair for

the deer hoofprints its legs leave. I try
to floss as much autumn through each
cornea as I can but it gunks up a cloud

scape somehow more solid on the face
of the lake. Light's a little too tacky for
another coat of Tuesday so we cut out

the corners, edge in the windows, and
wait, a Wednesday's on its way or will be.
Cold wind in the oak's got the sound

of summer rain down to a tree. Shoulder
of the road home the raw carcass of a deer
uncovered by crows flutters up a deck

of cards and we're all in. The only trick
my dog ever needed me to know was
hold up.

The Apricot Jelly Elegies

"Everything changes,
nothing perishes."

— Ovid, *Metamorphoses*

The rural lures real morning up
with nothing, just stink bait and song,

son-in-law and sonnet. But a clap
track can't make a dance mix, a star

collapse into an asterisk. Last night
before bed I read a little about how

now even electrons have tiny bits of
consciousness, also made the mistake

of reading though not really
understanding speech droplet studies

on dispersal in casual conversation.
Little spit might not have much mind

to make up but I bet there's a question,
a line of inquiry to get in this reliquary

a mile long. What's it want? Warm wet
hole same as most, a host, night out

in the gladdening crowd. It took this
mask for me to kiss myself at last

good-bye and I know I'm probably
not safe until my phone stops auto

correcting to Ovid 19. Replication
and mutation, the botch and the copy,

faithfulness and fraternity house Gen
Ed final exam answer bank. Best part

of this virus is you keep singing
the same tune and still mean every

word, some of which is sepulcher
jangle, some fawn spot tree bark.

That high up the neck this early in
the solo, so now how low you go,

how slow is the song. Just one minute
of singing detonates a thousand

droplets but luckily this poem's
almost done for. Sparrows scatter

from the bottom of the bushes, look
like someone's footsteps coming

down the walk, but slow-mo
blown-up into the air and away.

All The Folks Agree That This Is Terrible

Someone told me the story of a man
about to be executed asking for a single
olive with a pit for his final meal, so
an olive tree might grow from his remains.

I always fall a little in love with anyone
who tells me stories like that. The warden
told him about his own stomach acid,
the furnace and grounds crew with riding

mowers, the nothing but clouds and very little
rain on unmarked graves. It's therapy for me,
born prematurely, lying on the floor chewing
gum to wad with balloon string and putty into

my belly button, the balloon above me barely
kissing ceiling. I remember I had a few songs
in the juke box still, if you know what I mean.
I mean my mother. Let me start over. I can

still hear Herbert Morrison from WLS radio
in Chicago calling in the Hindenberg,
the last thing he isn't always screaming it
is practically standing still.

Same Pajamas, but Everything Else Changes
(Revision as Recurring Dream)

Since we stepped back through the puddle club everything lightheads, effervesces, carbonates into this fizz of butter-colored moths up and around englobing us, interrupted from the mud they sip for minerals. Raptor shadow right overhead but nowhere in the sky, I tried, must've gone back inside the sun. Meanwhile I did these little inlays in the morning out of toast. You like that? From here on all topics are studies and all studies, topics. It's the final frontier we can't yet imagine. It's not rayguns. It's Walgreen's. It took the streetlit dark last night to see the leaves were changing while we were waiting. First autumn morning and the sun opens with its moon cover, then some new thing, and the trees yellow the light a little more each day. It works a lot like moonlight—it isn't, but still, it's still. Even that stone dead oak's got way more going on than me, the whole thing's in shadow but two antennae poking into dawn, a woodpecker each. I don't like it when a light flickers in a parking lot, gas station, or store, there's too much info in it. But it's okay it's my brain and I'm gouging at it deep down cold into the case with an ice cream scoop and all you asked for was a taste and now escape but wait you haven't tried the sky over the orchard yet late summer afternoon peak in the wave pool of this old school graveyard. Can I help whoever's last? Which apple's got that sweet silver underleaf? Ever see a hound stir pink dust from strictus, which I'd have called red thistle gone to seed if they'd asked me that day I'd say first frost the cake plate please give it something to hang onto because we're coming in dancing.

The Sound of Slowly Torn Up Grass for Grace

A hundred sacral pops
from tiny spines
find her the chiropractor
and we're all just late
for an adjustment.
Was that one of us
screaming? Our life's
a problem of our own
design, so at least
we know it's sound.
She goes to the lake to
really just see it through
the trees and leaves.
But at the park she
tears a little harder
at her everything bagel
to be sure to shed a lot
of seeds for the sparrows.
In the world of ten thousand
strings she's trying to
come up with something.
What flower does it
come from, that birdsong,
what scent that throat?
Now the cat knows where
the bunnies burrow, or
used to, she always carries
a crumpled-up piece
of paper, writes
the same psalm
over and over:
when hydrogen atoms
fuse into helium
in the furnace of
the sun, it can take
ten million years

to climb to the surface
and then it's nine
more minutes to us
down here where
luckily our aloes grow
mostly at the rate
we burn.

If there's a last minute snafu
at the planetarium, up there
where there's nothing but cold

and collision in collusion to create
and destroy every single explicable
blip of this shit, let's you and I

meet outside under one more
stocked summer sky, somewhere
in between a car port and garage,

a trickle and barrage, a blab, a button
up, a slap and a psalm and Ptolomy
and P.T. Barnum, pterodactyls

we'll resemble. That cloud's
a beard and that one's a skull
and they're off in two different

directions, but in want of one
face, one window where right
now starlight fires a few billion

frontal lobes, maybe less, and
of those less printers than you'd
guess, going: *Outer fucking space,*

prune of gritty nothing, only all
at once in the mystical moist
night air. The newest truth's

its vacuum even weighs something.
They say 40 tons of dust fall
to earth each day. It's okay.

Keep your pages open a little
while longer. We don't need to
not be someplace.

Tricycle

If you line it up right
walking west again
up the alley toward

Greenwood School,
for eight or nine strides
its rusted-stuck weathervane

seems to spell out SEWN,
so the fabric of the world
meets up again here—

South East West North,
this high hide of sky
I'd hem to hold together

had I any other thread
than this. Every bike
gets walked away from.

Morning does orange
chalk down low so
the little ones can

color, too, but up high
it's varsity blue.
All day the moon

makes due on powdered
milk. Rusted ten speed
leans I guess an eleventh

against an old garage.
I already miss you
was how we met.

Last Six Hrs. of Summer

I used to be one of the only suspicious
persons in the neighborhood, now everything's
specialization. My boss would like a Ferrari
the color of that dragonfly, but luckily I am
unemployed. Dew in the webs spun into
the grass like topographic maps of breath
all across the lawn—it's imaging, it's imagining
a slopescape morning run aground on somehow
just these anchored grafts, these staked-down
clouds sliced right off our skin of sky. What time
of year is this really? The old road's new loud
limestone load talcums the grass and yellow
maples all the way into town now in mortuary
fog. Along the creek, then back and down,
around and past that left ventricle of a duplex
on Buchanan with the cross spray-painted on
the door, then spray-painted back out in a blot,
the black and white cat out back, skinny and
seated and right where they left, street number
109 stuck mid-stumble, so it's almost 106
or will be when it swings all the way down
on that one last nail, one more slammed door.
And what day is it? The little pile of stones
won't say, won't budge from the two-year old
calendar waterlogged on the stairs, at least until
I get as brave as I am curious to count them off
and see some weeks and months and hope
what, a day's circled? There's a star? Three
hearts? An X? An answer? Blacked-out square?
A spray-painted season? What is time but
twelve soaked months of inspirational quotes
under some rocks, two handfuls at most?
What am I going to read their mail? Mine's
just down the drive if I get any braver than I
am right now. It's not flight or fight it's and,
it's so and it's ampersand, so also it's equals,
it is is is is is is.

Did You Get My Email?

A few more days of fall and all
cardinals could fly these red maples
naked and we'd never know. A lot

of what we don't know we never
will, but we've such lousy recall
it all feels like we're learning.

End of summer's riled bulb
is a lurid ebb of bluebirds, a rubbed
up bride's lubed bible. O, System

Administrator, everything's over
its size limit. The sky's inbox
of cloud, mosquito's inbox of blood,

my mouth's sent items. Only
the most practiced marching bands
know just how far away to stay

from one another. Are we merely
enacting singularity's rapid expansion
or are we more void adroit than

that? Are we even checking our email
like a look into a port-a-potty,
deep stewed blue pool on which

seems to float a face? Hey gorgeous,
disgorge us. In the beginning,
a benign egg bingeing gin.

At the start, not art, but rot,
tear tar. From the jump comes
plummet, and from the tongue

the tune goes out toward eon's
tug. Just wait a minute and the bang
keeps getting bigger.

New Lang Syne

The one year I wore a watch
took forever. It was always
tomorrow anytime someone
made eggs. Clouds threw
everything they had at us.
Each sun went down quick,
but left these freckles. Maybe
the shapes of the vapors
showed up in the papers.
Sunday's sad lattice of light
and shade. OK you can go
back to the past with all you
know now, but know everyone
else back there then now
knows, too. The advantage
was always this vantage, age,
invented vintage. Now
they're all back with what
they've been through, too.
The past insists it comes
to this, just not yet. Now
my dog and me watch
the park crew hang up
bunting on the outfield fence
for what must be a playoff
game, although it seems
a little early in the summer
to get sent home. It's good
to prepare for the past.
It's back there. All it wants
is in. But no one's going to
leave so it's got to wait.

This Much

Sunrise needs more glass in its diet
so I'm up in the kitchen to window it.
If my pencil lead's not soft enough
it'll outlive me. If you're not part
pollinator, you're part of the problem.
The garden's going to golden, go
down on one knee in a lean and then
brown out in a mush of November
rain, and mulch the sepulcher of earth
to raise again come spring rot's tots.
Something big and rotten's always
beeping back up our streets. Tuesdays,
at least. Unless the schedule's knocked
off its moorings by a holiday and what's
more holy than a toppled mooring? I am
ten seconds away from getting up to
figure out those tiny neon flowers
out there colored lipstick long-term
maternity leave choir sub. Mouths
fly out a voice. Every time I see
a red-tailed hawk I get a paper cut
later that day. Hurts like a nine but
I've always been a cry baby five.
I'm scared this much but I care this
much. If you have a heart in your chest
Act I come Act II some damn fool's
going to get himself loved. Look,
I already told you. Hello.

Acknowledgments

My thanks to the editors and readers of the magazines in which some of these poems first appeared.

Bear Review: "Prairie Warble"
Cimarron Review: "Besos de los Perros"
Diagram: "Among the Attributes of a Basically Cruel Man,"
"Iron-Clad Lullaby,"
Forklift, Ohio: "The Sound of Slowly Torn Up Grass for Grace,"
"Did You Get My Email?"
Ninth Letter: "Out Into the Worldness I Did Roam,"
"The Goldfinch Caution Tapes"
The Laurel Review: "New Lang Syne," "Please Come"
Mississippi Review: "Kindled Measures Going Out"
South Dakota Review: "Estados Unidos,"
Sprung Formal: "Quantum Tantrum,"
"Self-Portrait as Isaac Newton in Quarantine"

And to the editors and readers of the chapbook series in which some versions first appeared:

Diagram / New Michigan: *Slur Oeuvre*
CutBank Books: *Weathermanic*
Wells College Press: *This Much*
Ghost City Press: *Evolutionary Aesthetic Safeguard*

*

"Attack Decay Sustain Release" is for Barry Phipps
"The Sound of Slowly Torn Up Grass for Grace" is for Grace Olivialarae
"You Are" is for Alan Smith
"Iron-Clad Lullaby" is for Aaron Fine
"All The Folks Agree That This Is Terrible" is for CAConrad
"Tricycle" is for Troy Paino
"Apricot Jelly Elegies" is for Dereck Daschke
"If You Ever See My Soul Walking Down the Street You Better Cross to the Other Side of Heaven" is for James Cianciola

"Please Come" is for Derrick Rohr

*

For support during, after, and especially, before these poems were ever written: Dean Young, Nancy Eimers, Bill Olsen, Mary Ruefle, David Wojahn, Roger Mitchell, Ander Monson, Dan Rosenberg, Ron Mohring, Stephen Furlong, Brad Smith, Phil Schaefer, Aura Martin, Monica Fallone, Robyn Schroeder, SG Maldonado-Vélez, Sujash Purna, Rae Doyle, Claire Hoffman, Zoe Hitzel, Alan Smith, Katie Holtmeyer, Michael Derby, John Gibbs, Cassie Duggan, Andrew Kindiger, Alex Ewing, Leia Penina Wilson, Kimmy Walters, Shawn Bodden, Kirk Schleuter, Kasey Perkins, Kate Hawkins, Tori Hudson, Alex Wennerberg, Sad Joy Sullivan, Cole Piedimonte, Kim Ramos, Caroline Taylor, Zoe Aldrich, Sam Gran, Grace Mohler, Quinn Prouty, Anna Meister, Derrick Rohr, Rachelle Wales, Kristina Kohl, Lin Godfrey, Robby Garner, Ray Holmes, Drew Turner, Franklin Cline, Katie Walker, Carly Winchell, Megan Matheney, Jen Creer, Christian Hatala, McKinley Reshamwala, Zeeshan Reshamwala, Natalie Schmickley, Connor Robison, Ian Wohlstadter, Jordan LaBarge, Jimmy Sorsen, John Gallaher, Daniel Biegelson, Adam Clay, Timothy Green, Matt Mauch, Maryfrances Wagner, Greg Field, Hadara Bar Nadav, Jordan Stempleman, Christopher Nelson, Jocelyn Cullity, Monica Barron, Joe Benevento, Adam Davis, Brian Heston, Karen Kubin, Royce Kallerud, Aaron Fine, Luke Amoroso, Dave Lusk, JR, Troy Paino, Kelly Paino, Sue Thomas, Julia DeLancey, Pete Kelly, Dereck Daschke, Wendy Miner, Rebecca Dierking, Lisa Goran, Jason Luscier, Barbara Price, Jared Young, Chris Lindley, Tim Barcus, Taylor Byington, Mary Poe Smith, Sara Sauers, Mike Lewis-Beck, Sara Langworthy, Kory Stiffler, Julie Leonard, Giselle Simón, Barry Phipps, Sagan, Claire Peckosh, Debbie Downs, Alex Tetlak, Bridget Thomas, James Cianciola, Heather Cianciola, Vivian Valentine, JRB, Joan Carcia, Peter Carcia, Amanda Nadelberg, Matt Hart, Dobby Gibson, and Karen Carcia.

A Note About the Author

James D'Agostino is the author of *Nude With Anything* (New Issues Press), and three chapbooks which won prizes from Diagram/New Michigan, CutBank Books, and Wells College Press. His chapbook, *Gorilla by Jellyfish Light*, is forthcoming from Seven Kitchens Press. His poems have appeared in *Ninth Letter*, *Forklift Ohio*, *Conduit*, *Mississippi Review*, *Bear Review*, *TriQuarterly*, *Laurel Review*, and elsewhere. He teaches at Truman State University, lives in Missouri and Iowa City, Iowa, with his partner, the poet and book artist Karen Carcia.

A Note About the Anthony Hecht Poetry Prize

The Anthony Hecht Poetry Prize was inaugurated in 2005 and is awarded on an annual basis to the best first or second collection of poems submitted.

FIRST ANNUAL HECHT PRIZE
Judge: J. D. McClatchy
Winner: Morri Creech, *Field Knowledge*

SECOND ANNUAL HECHT PRIZE
Judge: Mary Jo Salter
Winner: Erica Dawson, *Big-Eyed Afraid*

THIRD ANNUAL HECHT PRIZE
Judge: Richard Wilbur
Winner: Rose Kelleher, *Bundle o' Tinder*

FOURTH ANNUAL HECHT PRIZE
Judge: Alan Shapiro
Winner: Carrie Jerrell, *After the Revival*

FIFTH ANNUAL HECHT PRIZE
Judge: Rosanna Warren
Winner: Matthew Ladd, *The Book of Emblems*

SIXTH ANNUAL HECHT PRIZE
Judge: James Fenton
Winner: Mark Kraushaar, *The Uncertainty Principle*

SEVENTH ANNUAL HECHT PRIZE
Judge: Mark Strand
Winner: Chris Andrews, *Lime Green Chair*

EIGHTH ANNUAL HECHT PRIZE
Judge: Charles Simic
Winner: Shelley Puhak, *Guinevere in Baltimore*

NINTH ANNUAL HECHT PRIZE
Judge: Heather McHugh
Winner: Geoffrey Brock, *Voices Bright Flags*

TENTH ANNUAL HECHT PRIZE
Judge: Anthony Thwaite
Winner: Jaimee Hills, *How to Avoid Speaking*

ELEVENTH ANNUAL HECHT PRIZE
Judge: Eavan Boland
Winner: Austin Allen, *Pleasures of the Game*

TWELFTH ANNUAL HECHT PRIZE
Judge: Gjertrud Schnackenberg
Winner: Mike White, *Addendum to a Miracle*

THIRTEENTH ANNUAL HECHT PRIZE
Judge: Andrew Motion
Winner: Christopher Cessac, *The Youngest Ocean*

FOURTEENTH ANNUAL HECHT PRIZE
Judge: Charles Wright
Winner: Katherine Hollander, *My German Dictionary*

FIFTEENTH ANNUAL HECHT PRIZE
Judge: Edward Hirsch
Winner: James Davis, *Club Q*

SIXTEENTH ANNUAL HECHT PRIZE
Judge: Vijay Seshadri
Winner: Danielle Blau, *peep*

SEVENTEENTH ANNUAL HECHT PRIZE
Judge: Alice Fulton
Winner: James D'Agostino, *The Goldfinch Caution Tapes*

Other Books from Waywiser

POETRY

Austin Allen, *Pleasures of the Game*
Al Alvarez, *New & Selected Poems*
Chris Andrews, *Lime Green Chair*
Danielle Blau, *peep*
Audrey Bohanan, *Any Keep or Contour*
George Bradley, *A Few of Her Secrets*
Geoffrey Brock, *Voices Bright Flags*
Christopher Cessac, *The Youngest Ocean*
Robert Conquest, *Blokelore & Blokesongs*
Robert Conquest, *Collected Poems*
Robert Conquest, *Penultimata*
Morri Creech, *Blue Rooms*
Morri Creech, *Field Knowledge*
Morri Creech, *The Sleep of Reason*
Peter Dale, *One Another*
James Davis, *Club Q*
Erica Dawson, *Big-Eyed Afraid*
B. H. Fairchild, *The Art of the Lathe*
David Ferry, *On This Side of the River: Selected Poems*
Daniel Groves & Greg Williamson, eds., *Jiggery-Pokery Semicentennial*
Jeffrey Harrison, *The Names of Things: New & Selected Poems*
Joseph Harrison, *Identity Theft*
Joseph Harrison, *Shakespeare's Horse*
Joseph Harrison, *Someone Else's Name*
Joseph Harrison, *Sometimes I Dream That I Am Not Walt Whitman*
Joseph Harrison, ed., *The Hecht Prize Anthology, 2005-2009*
Anthony Hecht, *Collected Later Poems*
Anthony Hecht, *The Darkness and the Light*
Jaimee Hills, *How to Avoid Speaking*
Katherine Hollander, *My German Dictionary*
Hilary S. Jacqmin, *Missing Persons*
Carrie Jerrell, *After the Revival*
Stephen Kampa, *Articulate as Rain*
Stephen Kampa, *Bachelor Pad*
Rose Kelleher, *Bundle o' Tinder*
Mark Kraushaar, *The Uncertainty Principle*
Matthew Ladd, *The Book of Emblems*
William Logan, *Old Flame: New Selected Poems, 1974–2012*
J. D. McClatchy, *Plundered Hearts: New and Selected Poems*
Dora Malech, *Shore Ordered Ocean*
Jérôme Luc Martin, *The Gardening Fires: Sonnets and Fragments*
Eric McHenry, *Odd Evening*
Eric McHenry, *Potscrubber Lullabies*
Eric McHenry and Nicholas Garland, *Mommy Daddy Evan Sage*
Timothy Murphy, *Very Far North*
Ian Parks, *Shell Island*
V. Penelope Pelizzon, *Whose Flesh is Flame, Whose Bone is Time*

Other Books from Waywiser

Chris Preddle, *Cattle Console Him*
Shelley Puhak, *Guinevere in Baltimore*
Christopher Ricks, ed., *Joining Music with Reason:*
34 Poets, British and American, Oxford 2004-2009
Daniel Rifenburgh, *Advent*
Mary Jo Salter, *It's Hard to Say: Selected Poems*
W. D. Snodgrass, *Not for Specialists: New & Selected Poems*
Mark Strand, *Almost Invisible*
Mark Strand, *Blizzard of One*
Bradford Gray Telford, *Perfect Hurt*
Matthew Thorburn, *This Time Tomorrow*
Cody Walker, *Shuffle and Breakdown*
Cody Walker, *The Self-Styled No-Child*
Cody Walker, *The Trumpiad*
Henry Walters, *The Nature Thief*
Deborah Warren, *The Size of Happiness*
Clive Watkins, *Already the Flames*
Clive Watkins, *Jigsaw*
Richard Wilbur, *Anterooms*
Richard Wilbur, *Mayflies*
Richard Wilbur, *Collected Poems 1943-2004*
Norman Williams, *One Unblinking Eye*
Greg Williamson, *A Most Marvelous Piece of Luck*
Greg Williamson, *The Hole Story of Kirby the Sneak and Arlo the True*
Stephen Yenser, *Stone Fruit*

FICTION
Gregory Heath, *The Entire Animal*
Mary Elizabeth Pope, *Divining Venus*
K. M. Ross, *The Blinding Walk*
Gabriel Roth, *The Unknowns**
Matthew Yorke, *Chancing It*

ILLUSTRATED
Nicholas Garland, *I wish ...*
Eric McHenry and Nicholas Garland, *Mommy Daddy Evan Sage*
Greg Williamson, *The Hole Story of Kirby the Sneak and Arlo the True*

NON-FICTION
Neil Berry, *Articles of Faith: The Story of British Intellectual Journalism*
Irving Feldman, *Usable Truths: Aphorisms & Observations*
Mark Ford, *A Driftwood Altar: Essays and Reviews*
Philip Hoy, *M. Degas Steps Out*
Philip Hoy, ed., *A Bountiful Harvest: The Correspondence of Anthony Hecht and William L. MacDonald*
John Rosenthal, *Searching for Amylu Danzer*
Richard Wollheim, *Germs: A Memoir of Childhood*

*Co-published with Picador